PIP AND BUNNY: PIP AT HOME

The invaluable 'Pip and Bunny' collection is a set of six picture books with an accompanying handbook and e-resources carefully written and illustrated to support the development of visual and literary skills. By inspiring conversation and imagination, the books promote emotional and social literacy in the young reader.

Designed for use within the early years setting or at home, each story explores different areas of social and emotional development. The full set includes:

- six beautifully illustrated picture books with text and vocabulary for each
- a handbook designed to guide the adult in using the books effectively
- 'Talking Points' relating to the child's own world
- 'What's the Word?' picture pages to be photocopied, downloaded or printed for language development
- detailed suggestions as to how to link with other EYFS areas of learning.

The set is designed to be used in both individual and group settings. It will be a valuable resource for teachers, SENCOs (preschool and reception), Early Years Staff (nursery, preschool and reception), EOTAs, Educational Psychologists, Counsellors and Speech Therapists.

Maureen Glynn has 25 years' experience teaching primary and secondary age children in mainstream, home school and special school settings, in the UK and Ireland.

First published 2020
by Routledge
2 Park Square, Milton Park, Abingdon, Oxon OX14 4RN

and by Routledge
52 Vanderbilt Avenue, New York, NY 10017

Routledge is an imprint of the Taylor & Francis Group, an informa business

British Library Cataloguing-in-Publication Data
A catalogue record for this book is available from the British Library

Library of Congress Cataloging-in-Publication Data
A catalog record for this book has been requested

ISBN: 978-0-367-19110-8 (pbk)
ISBN: 978-0-429-35499-1 (ebk)

Typeset in Calibri
by Apex CoVantage, LLC

Visit www.Routledge.com/9780367136642

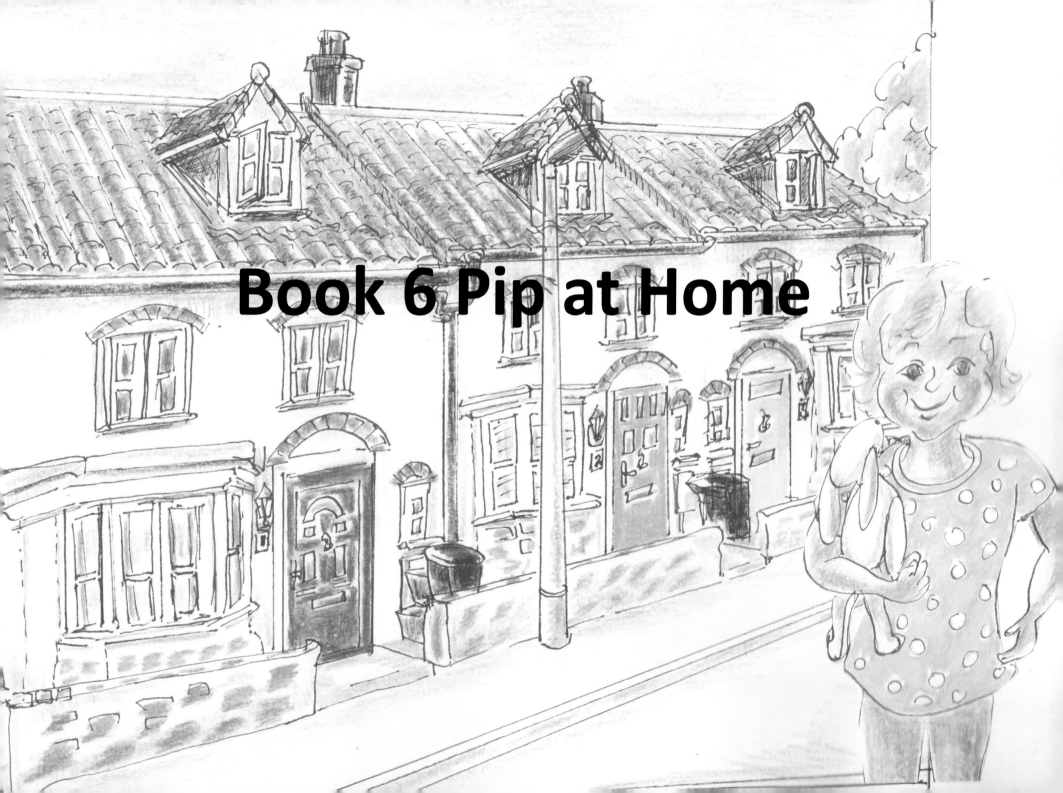

Book 6 Pip at Home

Pip loves her home where she lives
with Mummy and Daddy and Bunny.
Their home is a terraced house.
Each door in the street is a different colour.

There is so much to do at home.

Pip loves to listen to stories
with Bunny.
They look at the pictures and
follow some of the words.

They play games indoors.

Pip knows all the best places to hide.

Mummy or Daddy count to ten slowly and then
try to find her.

Pip then counts and tries to find them.

Sometimes Pip and her cousins
or friends dress up.
They are beautiful princesses, a clever wizard
or a wicked witch...

a cruel pirate or a Red Indian running around the garden.

In her garden, Pip likes to water the flowers and make petal potions in a jug.

Beside the shed, Pip suddenly screams with pain.

She screams and screams and cries. It hurts so much!

Daddy carries her indoors.
'What's happened?' he asks.
He sees a nasty red sore on her leg.
'That's a bee sting!' he exclaims.

First he pulls out the sting with
tweezers.
He soothes the sore with cold
water and dabs it dry.
Then he applies magic cream.
'That will make it better!' he
says, giving Pip a hug.

When Tommy falls over into the nettle patch, he gets stung too.

Pip wants to help.

She thinks and then she says to him,

'I know!...

a dock leaf and magic cream will make it better!'

Today it is raining.

Pip helps Mummy to make flapjacks in the kitchen.

They use oats, golden syrup, butter and a few raisins.

Pip washes her hands because the syrup is so sticky.
But the water is too hot. Oh no!
She burns her finger. That hurts too!
Cold water helps to cool the pain.

When the flapjacks are baked and
ready to eat,
Pip enjoys a square with Bunny.
It tastes delicious!
She feels much better now.

Book 6 Pip at Home What's the Word?

Show the page and ask the child to say words that explain each image:

Page 17 Action Words?

Page 18 Location Words?

Page 19 Descriptive Words?

Page 20 Home Words?

Page 21 Emotions and Feelings?

Action Words?

Location Words?

Descriptive Words?

Home Words?

Emotions and Feelings?